Did You Know? WILTSHIRE

A MISCELLANY

Compiled by Julia Skinner

With particular reference to the work of Dee La Vardera, Les Moores and Dennis Needham

THE FRANCIS FRITH COLLECTION

www.francisfrith.com

First published in the United Kingdom in 2013 by The Francis Frith Collection®

This edition published exclusively for Bradwell Books in 2013
For trade enquiries see: www.bradwellbooks.com or tel: 0800 834 920
ISBN 978-1-84589-740-6

Text and Design copyright The Francis Frith Collection®
Photographs copyright The Francis Frith Collection® except where indicated.

The Frith® photographs and the Frith® logo are reproduced under licence from
Heritage Photographic Resources Ltd, the owners of the Frith® archive and trademarks.
'The Francis Frith Collection', 'Francis Frith' and 'Frith' are registered trademarks of
Heritage Photographic Resources Ltd.

All rights reserved. No photograph in this publication may be sold to a third party other than in the
original form of this publication, or framed for sale to a third party. No parts of this publication may be
reproduced, stored in a retrieval system, or transmitted, in any form, or by any means, electronic, mechanical,
photocopying, recording or otherwise, without the prior permission of the publishers and copyright holder.

British Library Cataloguing in Publication Data

Did You Know? Wiltshire - A Miscellany
Compiled by Julia Skinner
With particular reference to the work of Dee La Vardera, Les Moores and Dennis Needham

The Francis Frith Collection
6 Oakley Business Park,
Wylye Road, Dinton,
Wiltshire SP3 5EU
Tel: +44 (0) 1722 716 376
Email: info@francisfrith.co.uk
www.francisfrith.com

Printed and bound in Malaysia
Contains material sourced from responsibly managed forests

Front Cover: **CASTLE COMBE, THE VILLAGE 1904** 51508p
Frontispiece: **SALISBURY, HIGH STREET 1919** 68969
Contents: **ERLESTOKE, THE VILLAGE 1900** 45360

The colour-tinting is for illustrative purposes only, and is not intended to be historically accurate

AS WITH ANY HISTORICAL DATABASE, THE FRANCIS FRITH ARCHIVE IS CONSTANTLY BEING
CORRECTED AND IMPROVED, AND THE PUBLISHERS WOULD WELCOME INFORMATION ON
OMISSIONS OR INACCURACIES

CONTENTS

2 Introduction
4 Wiltshire Dialect Words and Phrases
5 Haunted Wiltshire
6 Wiltshire Miscellany
46 Sporting Wiltshire
48 Quiz Questions
50 Recipes
52 Quiz Answers
54 Francis Frith - Pioneer Victorian Photographer

Did You Know?
WILTSHIRE
A MISCELLANY

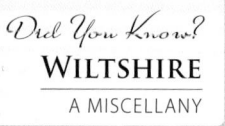

INTRODUCTION

From the commercial bustle of modern, vibrant Swindon, historic Salisbury and scattered market towns to sleepy, archetypal English villages, Wiltshire is a county of contrasts – so much so, in fact, that its landscape has given us the expression 'as different as chalk and cheese', referring to the difference between the chalk uplands to the south and east of the county, where huge flocks of sheep used to graze in the past, and the fertile, lush country to the north and west with their dairy farms.

Wiltshire is a long, rectangular-shaped county, which is some 50 miles long and 30 miles wide at its broadest point and includes much of the huge area of chalk plateau known as Salisbury Plain, a large part of which is occupied by the British Army as its main training area in the UK. The Plain not only dominates but also divides the county in many ways, particularly because it forms a natural central barrier which keeps communities apart. The other areas of unspoilt downland, near Marlborough and along the Chalke and Nadder river valleys, are sparsely populated but filled with small villages and towns. Wiltshire's whole character as a county is wrapped up in its unique river system: the Bristol Avon (which flows through Wiltshire from Malmesbury to Bradford-on-Avon), the Salisbury Avon, and the valleys of the Kennet, Nadder, Wylye, Ebble and Bourne, all running west to east. These pretty valleys and the majestic downs are stark in contrast but abundantly attractive to inhabitants and visitors. Large wooded areas in some parts of the county also add to the rich countryside inheritance that is Wiltshire. The small valley towns make up most of the population of the county, which was estimated at 639,500 in the 2011 Census. Wiltshire's only city is Salisbury, but the largest conurbation is Swindon. The county town is Trowbridge, the seat of Wiltshire Council.

Did You Know?
WILTSHIRE
A MISCELLANY

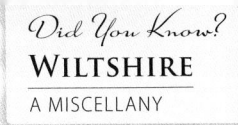

The traditional nickname of 'Moonrakers' for Wiltshire folk derives from the county's widespread smuggling trade of the 18th and 19th centuries, when illicit goods landed on the Dorset and Hampshire coast were transported across the county to Swindon, which was a major distribution centre for the contraband, from where it was transported further north. The story goes that on the night of a full moon, some men from Bishops Cannings were transporting smuggled kegs of brandy hidden in a wagon-load of hay when they heard the Devizes Excisemen approaching. They quickly extracted the kegs and threw them into a nearby pond. The Excisemen were put off, but not fooled – they left, but doubled back to discover the smugglers attempting to recover the submerged kegs with hay rakes. When they were asked what they were doing, the countrymen indicated the clear reflection of the full moon shining in the water like a great golden cheese and uttered something like 'Zomebody 'ave lost thic thur cheese and we'm a-rakin for un in thic thur pond'. The Excisemen smiled at the country simpletons and went on their way, leaving the moonrakers free to go home – and enjoy their brandy. The story of 'The Wiltshire Moonrakers' is told in a long poem by the Wiltshire dialect poet Edward Slow (1841-1925), which ends:

> *Zoo, wen out thease County you da goo,*
> *An voke da poke ther vun at you;*
> *An caal ee a girt Willsheer coon,*
> *As went a reakun var tha moon*
> *Jist menshin thease yer leetle stowry,*
> *And then bust out in ael yer glowry,*
> *That, yer cute Excisemen vrum tha town,*
> *Wur took in wie a Willsheer clown.*
> *Zoo dwoant ee mine be'n call'd a Mooney,*
> *Twur he, ya zee, as wur tha Spooney.*

Wiltshire Dialect Words and Phrases

'A day back agone' – some time ago, in the past.

'Cack handed' – left handed, or clumsy.

'Chuckypigs', **'chuggypigs'** or **'grampfywigs'** – woodlice.

'Dumbledore' – a bumble bee.

'Emmet' – an ant.

'Gert' – big, large.

'Loppity' – feeling ill, run-down, under the weather.

'Nammet' – the mid-day snack.

'Narration' – a fuss, or commotion.

'Shrammed' – chilled to the bone.

'Somewhen' – some time.

'Spadgers' – sparrows.

'Teg' – a sheep, thus a **'tegman'** is a shepherd.

'Ther thee bist' – there you are.

'Vamplets' – gaiters.

'Where's it to?' – where is it?

'Yertiz' – here it is.

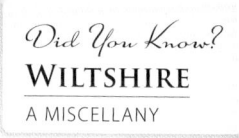

HAUNTED WILTSHIRE

One of Wiltshire's most impressive ancient monuments is the West Kennet Long Barrow, a Neolithic chambered tomb situated just south of the A4 between Marlborough and Beckhampton, which dates back to around 3,400BC. It is around 330ft (100m) long by around 66ft (20m) wide, making it one of the longest prehistoric barrows in Britain. Excavations in the 1950s discovered the remains of between 40 to 50 people inside the barrow, which is made up of five burial chambers set laterally either side of a corridor, with the largest chamber situated at the far western end. A number of eerie tales are linked with this ancient place, but the most famous is that at dawn on the summer solstice, 21st June, the ghostly figure of a man dressed in flowing white robes is said to stand on top of the eastern end of the mound, accompanied by a large hound with fiery red eyes. They stand motionless as they await the sunrise – then at first light, they turn and make their way to the entrance to the tomb, where they disappear inside….

Not far from Tisbury in south Wiltshire are the romantic ruins of Wardour Castle, off the A30 west of Salisbury, which was the home of the Arundell family during the Civil War. On 2nd May 1643 the castle came under attack by 1,300 Parliamentarian forces, defended only by 61-year-old Lady Blanche Arundell, a few maid-servants and just 25 fighting men. They held out until 8th May, before Lady Blanche was forced to surrender. She was kept prisoner for a while before being released, and then retreated to a life of seclusion in Winchester, where she died in 1649 – her son had managed to retake the castle in 1644, but it was left in ruins in the process. Lady Blanche was buried in St John's Church in Tisbury after her death, but her spirit seems to linger in the home she loved and fought so hard to defend – her ghost is said to roam the ruins to this day, especially at dusk, when her apparition walks across the grounds of the castle towards the nearby lake.

WILTSHIRE MISCELLANY

Wiltshire is named after the small town of Wilton, west of Salisbury, which was an important place in the past – it was the capital of 'Wiltunshire', a shire (or 'share') of the Anglo-Saxon kingdom of Wessex, and the administrative centre of the county until the 11th century. A famous king of Wessex was King Alfred the Great, who ruled from AD871 to 899 and whose statue stands in Pewsey, where he owned land. In the early years of his reign he fought a long struggle against the Viking Danes who were overrunning his kingdom, and in AD878, on the brink of defeat, he summoned the fighting men of Wessex for one last push against the Danes. A large force gathered to him and King Alfred and his army then defeated the Danes in a decisive victory at Edington, near Westbury in west Wiltshire. Legend suggests that the famous white horse chalk figure on the side of Bratton Hill near Westbury was originally carved out to commemorate the battle. The Westbury White Horse was re-cut in 1778 to be a better representation of a horse; originally it may have resembled the dragon-like White Horse of Uffington in Oxfordshire.

PEWSEY, THE KING ALFRED STATUE c1955 P51021

WESTBURY, THE WHITE HORSE 1900 45365

Did You Know?
WILTSHIRE
A MISCELLANY

A number of chalk figures cut out of the turf decorate Wiltshire's hillsides. These include more white horses, for example at Pewsey, Cherhill, Broad Hinton, Alton Barnes, Devizes and Marlborough (see www.wiltshirewhitehorses.org.uk for more information), a giant Kiwi bird on Beacon Hill above Bulford Camp on Salisbury Plain, which was cut by New Zealand soldiers awaiting repatriation after the First World War, and the series of regimental emblems along the A30 near Fovant in south Wiltshire, which also date from the First World War when a large military training and transit camp was established in the area. Over thirty regiments passed through it, many of which cut the emblems of their cap badges in the chalk. By the end of the war around 20 badges decorated the hillsides, although many no longer survive. Shortly after the Second World War the badge of the Wiltshire Regiment was also cut into the turf. The Fovant Badges Society maintains the remaining emblems as a memorial to all the soldiers who passed through the camp on their way to war, many never to return. For more information, or to make a donation towards their costly upkeep, see its website: www.fovantbadges.com

FOVANT, THE REGIMENTAL EMBLEMS 2013 F96709

South Wiltshire is the location of the famous prehistoric stone circle of Stonehenge. The monument was built and adapted in three phases over a huge time span, between approximately 2,950BC and 1,600BC. The first Stonehenge was a circular bank and ditch, probably containing timber uprights, then during the second phase (2,900-2,400BC), new timber settings were erected in the north-east entrance and at the centre. During these early phases it seems the purpose of the monument was the observation of the movements of the moon through the entrance, and it may also have been linked with death and funerary rituals. The Stonehenge we see today was developed in the third phase (2,550-1,600BC). The Hele Stone and another stone west of it were erected outside the monument pointing towards the approximate point where the midsummer sun rose. Bluestone pillars brought from the Preseli mountains in Wales were erected around the Altar Stone, then came a horseshoe-shaped setting of large trilithons. Surrounding these were more bluestones, then a ring of sarsen stones. The Avenue was also constructed at this time, connecting Stonehenge with the River Avon and aligned on the point of sunrise of the summer solstice, emphasising the change of observation from the moon to the sun.

Many people gather at Stonehenge each year to celebrate the summer solstice and watch the sun rise above the Hele Stone at dawn on the longest day of the year, 21st June. However, at some stage rituals marking the winter solstice were also important at Stonehenge, which may have been used for ceremonies to call back the sun at the darkest time of the year. Beyond the Hele Stone, 40 posts mark the axis of moonrise at the winter solstice, the shortest day of the year, 21st December. Even all that time ago, the ancient stargazers understood that the moon's position on the shortest day changes from year to year, over a lunar cycle of 18.61 years, and these posts marked all the positions. Four stones on the outer circle of the enclosure, known as Station Stones, also marked the intersection of lunar sight lines.

Did You Know?
WILTSHIRE
A MISCELLANY

This photograph looks southwards into Stonehenge from the Hele Stone. Through the middle arch, the tallest stone of the inner horseshoe of trilithons can be seen – it is topped with the oldest tenon joint in Britain, which would have been laboriously hammered out with football-shaped flint hammers. The lintel that originally capped this stone contained the mortise to hold it in place.

About two miles north-east of Stonehenge, just west of the A345 near Durrington, is the site of Woodhenge, a Neolithic henge and timber circle that was probably constructed between 2,470BC and 2,000BC, and used until around 1,800BC. Archaeological excavations of the site in the 1920s revealed 168 postholes within the ditched and banked enclosure of the circular henge, arranged in a pattern of six concentric oval rings; these originally held thick timber posts, and their positions are now marked with modern concrete posts. The crouched inhumation of a child was also found at the centre of the rings, which was interpreted as a dedicatory sacrifice.

STONEHENGE 1887 19796

Did You Know?
WILTSHIRE
A MISCELLANY

AVEBURY, THE DEVIL'S CHAIR c1908 A80303

Another important prehistoric site in Wiltshire is at Avebury, west of Marlborough, which is the largest Neolithic henge monument in Britain. It was completed by about 2,600BC. Avebury's massive bank and inner ditch encloses a circle of 98 sarsen stones, and within them were two smaller circles and a further setting of stones near the centre. (Sarsen stones are found in the nearby Marlborough downs, and are lumps of hard sandstone that were left after weather erosion of the chalk belt.) In prehistoric times there were four entrances into the henge marked by larger stones; these entrances are now used by modern roads, and some village houses at Avebury stand within the monument; these include the Red Lion pub, claimed to be the only pub in the world enclosed by a prehistoric stone circle! The massive stone seen in this view stands at the south entrance into the monument. There is a small, naturally formed, ledge on the outside of the stone (just behind the hat of the lady on the right) which can be used as a seat, hence its nickname of 'The Devil's Chair'.

In the Middle Ages the Church ordered that the Avebury stones were to be buried, to remove such pagan relics from the landscape. During excavation and restoration work at the ancient monument in 1938, a man's skeleton was discovered beneath one of the buried stones. Because his remains were found with some surgical tools as well as medieval coins, it is believed that the man was probably a barber-surgeon who died around 1330 when the stone fell on him during this work. The stone (in the south-west of the circle) has now been raised again and is known as the Barber's Stone.

One of Wiltshire's strangest prehistoric monuments is Silbury Hill, which lies beside the A4 a short distance south of Avebury, to the east of Beckhampton. It was constructed approximately 4,500 years ago and is the largest man-made mound in Europe. It covers an area of 5½ acres, and is 130ft (40m) high. Apart from its core and foundation layers of gravel, clay and soil, it is made entirely of chalk, excavated from the surrounding ditch. In 1883 Silbury Hill became the first site in Britain to be classified as an ancient monument, but its purpose remains a mystery. It was once thought to be a large burial mound for an important Bronze Age chieftain, but a number of archaeological excavations at the mound have failed to discover skeletal remains, or any other clues to what it was used for.

AVEBURY, SILBURY HILL c1955 A80011

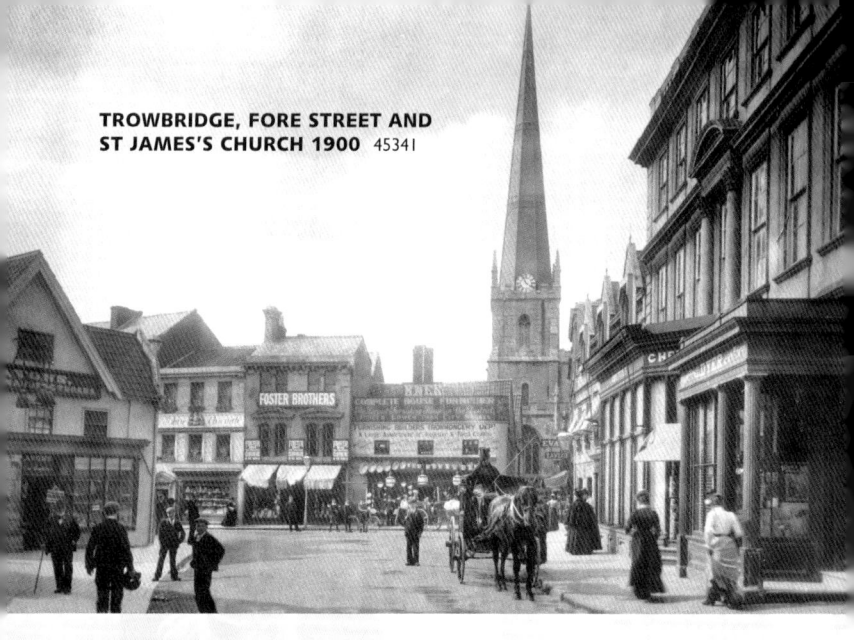

TROWBRIDGE, FORE STREET AND ST JAMES'S CHURCH 1900 45341

Wiltshire's county town and administrative centre is Trowbridge, with Wiltshire Council based at County Hall in Bythesea Road, named after a family of clothiers who once owned land in this part of town. Trowbridge was famous for its woollen cloth trade in the past, and many fine houses built by the wealthy cloth merchants still stand in the town, notably the palatial building that now houses the Lloyds Bank branch in Fore Street, which was built c1730 for the prominent clothier John Cooper. Trowbridge's historic cloth industry is recalled in several placenames in the modern town, such as Broadcloth Lane, Worsted Close and Ryeland Way, named after the Ryeland breed of sheep whose fleece provided wool for the early cloth mills. However, the industry was not without its troubles, as evidenced by the monument in St James's churchyard to 19-year-old apprentice shearman Thomas Helliker, who was executed in 1803 for leading a riot against the introduction of mechanised shearing frames that led to Littleton Mill at nearby Semington being burned down, despite having an alibi and protesting his innocence. Afterwards it was generally accepted that he had indeed been innocent, but although he knew the real culprits he refused to inform on them.

The odd brick building on the left of this view was the 'Handle House' for Studley Mill in Stallard Street in Trowbridge, known locally as Clarks Mill, which now houses the County Court. It was used for drying the flower heads of teasel plants – the holes in the brickwork of the building were to let air in and allow it to circulate. Teasels were used to raise the nap, or surface, of the material. This was done by drawing wooden frames set with teasel heads, called handles, over the dampened surface of the cloth. They were stored after use in buildings with ventilated walls. The Handle House at Trowbridge is the only certain example of such a building in the West of England woollen area.

Sir Isaac Pitman was born in Trowbridge in 1813, the son of a hand loom weaver. He was educated in the town and worked as a clerk in Court Mills before leaving Trowbridge to train as a teacher. He invented his 'stenographic sound hand' in 1837 during his teaching career – known nowadays as Pitman Shorthand.

TROWBRIDGE, THE HANDLE HOUSE, STUDLEY MILL
2004 T84712

This quaint building stands on the town bridge in Stallard Street in the centre of Trowbridge. It is a two-chambered 'lock-up', or town gaol, dated 1757, and is known as the Blind House because it has no windows, and therefore no one can see in or out. A number of similar local lock-ups are found elsewhere in Wiltshire, for example at Steeple Ashton, Bromham, Shrewton, Heytesbury, Hilperton, Luckington, Malmesbury, Warminster, Lacock, Box, and Bradford-on-Avon, a few miles north-west of Trowbridge.

TROWBRIDGE, THE BLIND HOUSE 2004 T84715

The nickname of 'Trowbridge Knobs' for Trowbridge people derives from the stone ball on top of the roof of the Blind House. Bradford-on-Avon people, on the other hand, are known as 'Bradford Gudgeons' after the fish emblem in the form of a gudgeon on the weather-vane on top of the lock-up on their town bridge. An old local saying describing occupants of the lock-up at Bradford-on-Avon was that they were 'under the fish and above the water'.

BRADFORD-ON-AVON, THE BRIDGE 1900 45374

BRADFORD-ON-AVON, ST LAURENCE'S CHURCH c1955 B174072

Bradford-on-Avon has one of the few almost complete Anglo-Saxon churches in England. St Laurence's Church in Church Street was probably built in the early 11th century, and the interior layout of this ancient church is remarkable for its tall, narrow proportions with small windows. This view gives a good sense of the height of the nave, with the very small chancel to the right. Inside the church, high above the chancel arch are two lovely carvings of angels set into the wall, which face each other across the arch opening.

From 1001 until 1539 the Bradford estate was a grange of Shaftesbury Abbey in Dorset, and the huge medieval tithe barn in Pound Lane at Bradford-on-Avon was where its produce was brought for storage. An impressive feature of its interior is the wonderful raised timber cruck roof, where a series of graceful wooden arches support the massive roofspan. Shaftesbury Abbey also had a grange at Tisbury in south Wiltshire, where the abbey's massive 15th-century tithe barn still stands at Place Farm, and has the largest thatched roof in the country.

Did You Know?
WILTSHIRE
A MISCELLANY

Melksham developed at a ford over the River Avon – its name probably derives from the Saxon 'meolchamm', meaning land in the bend of a river where milk is produced. Like many Wiltshire towns, for many centuries the main industry of Melksham was cloth weaving, but there were attempts to develop it as a spa town after saline and chalybeate springs were discovered there in 1815; this time in the town's history is recalled in the names of Spa Road and the area at the southern end of the town called The Spa, where the handsome three-storeyed stone houses built as lodging houses for the spa visitors still stand. A famous son of Melksham was John Fowler, the agricultural engineer and inventor, who was born there in 1826 and pioneered the use of first horse-drawn and then steam-driven drainage and ploughing machinery. His inventions enabled the drainage of previously uncultivated land, allowing it to be brought into agricultural production.

South-east of Melksham is Seend. When its parish church was rebuilt and enlarged in the 15th century, a wealthy local clothier called John Stokes funded the building of the north aisle; a reminder of what provided the money for this is the pair of clothier's shears carved into the window moulding above his memorial brass on the west wall.

The wool industry also dominated Calne for many centuries. The view of The Green on the opposite page shows some of the town's best Georgian buildings, with two fine examples of clothiers' houses on the right, which date from the mid 17th century and were re-fronted and altered in the late 18th century. The chemist Dr Joseph Priestley (1733-1804) and his family lived in a house on The Green for seven years in the 1770s whilst Priestley worked at nearby Bowood House, the seat of the Marquess of Lansdowne, as the librarian and tutor to the 1st Marquess's sons. It was in his laboratory at Bowood in 1774 that Dr Priestley discovered oxygen.

Did You Know?
WILTSHIRE
A MISCELLANY

In the 19th and 20th centuries the Harris factory was the most important business in Calne, producing bacon, ham, sausages and other pork products. In the background of this view is St Mary's Church which is famous for its giant five-manual organ, known as 'The Sausage Organ' because it was donated by Henry George Harris in 1908. It is the only organ of its kind in the south of England, and was awarded a certificate Grade II by the British Institute of Organ Studies in 2008 as an instrument of importance to the national heritage.

One of the most unusual churches in Wiltshire can be found at Sandy Lane, south-west of Calne, where the quaint Church of St Mary the Virgin and St Nicholas is a small timber building with a steep thatched roof. It was built to the design of J H Hopkins in 1892 as a mission church to the newly created parish of Chittoe and was originally dedicated to St Nicholas; it was rededicated with its present joint dedication in 1981.

CALNE, THE GREEN c1957 C228032

Did You Know?
WILTSHIRE
A MISCELLANY

North-west of Calne is Bremhill, where this monument on Wick Hill topped with a rustic seated figure of a woman with her basket commemorates Maud Heath, who lived nearby in the 15th-century and regularly carried butter and eggs over the muddy, uneven ground between her home and Chippenham to sell at the market. She died in 1474 and left a deed of gift for the income from her property to be used by a group of trustees to construct and maintain a proper footpath to Chippenham for local people to use. Maud Heath's Causeway begins at Wick Hill and then runs for four and a half miles through Tytherton, then goes across the River Avon to Kellaways, through Langley Burrell and into Chippenham at Langley Road, ending at the corner of Foundry Lane in the town. Some of it is now followed by modern roads and lanes, whilst in other places it forms a roadside pavement. The most famous section is where the causeway is carried over the flood plain of the River Avon on either side of the bridge at Kellaways on a course of 64 brick arches that were built by the trustees in 1811.

BREMHILL, MAUD HEATH MONUMENT
c1960 B375004

KELLAWAYS
THE MAUD HEATH CAUSEWAY
c1955 K224061

CHIPPENHAM, THE YELDE HALL c1965 C294104

Although there is evidence of settlement in the Chippenham area since before Roman times, the earliest documentary evidence for the town gives a date in the 9th century, during the Saxon period. The 'Anglo-Saxon Chronicle' records the town as 'Cippanhamme', and this could be derived from a personal name, Cippa, referring to Cippa's 'hamm', meaning an enclosure in a river meadow, or from 'Cheppeham', meaning a trading and market place. One of the few surviving medieval timber-framed buildings in the town is the Yelde Hall in the market place, which was constructed in the 15th century and originally used as a market with internal divisions. The hall and its upstairs room were used by the bailiff and burgesses for local government meetings. Underneath the chamber was the lock-up or blind house. An intriguing entry in the bailiff's accounts for 1709 records how he 'spent with 6 pirates in custody, one shilling for seven quarts of ale'. After serving many different roles over the years, the Yelde Hall is now part of the Chippenham Museums and Heritage Service and one of the town's most iconic buildings.

Did You Know? WILTSHIRE
A MISCELLANY

South of Chippenham is Lacock Abbey, originally an Augustinian nunnery founded in the 13th century. The abbey was closed down in 1539 by King Henry VIII and the site was bought by Sir William Sharington, who converted it into a private house; he demolished the abbey church, but the cloisters, sacristy, chapter house and monastic rooms of the abbey have survived largely intact. He also built the polygonal Sharington's Tower on the right of this view. After his death Lacock Abbey passed to his brother, Sir Henry Sharington. His daughter Olive fell in love with John Talbot, a younger brother of the Earl of Shrewsbury, but Sir Henry would not allow them to marry. One night Olive was on the roof of the tower talking to John down below, and decided to jump down to him so they could elope. He readied himself to catch her and down she leapt, but poor John was nearly killed when she landed on top of him. However, all ended happily. John regained consciousness to make a full recovery, and Olive's father had a change of heart, declaring that 'since she had made such a leap, she should e'en marrie him' – so she did.

LACOCK, THE ABBEY 1904 51510

Olive inherited the Lacock estate from her father, and Lacock Abbey passed down through the descendants of her marriage to John Talbot until Matilda Talbot gave it to the National Trust in 1944. One of those descendants was the inventor and pioneer photographer William Henry Fox Talbot, who lived at Lacock Abbey from 1800 to 1877, and whose work laid the foundations of modern photography. Talbot's importance is that he established the basis of the photographic process that is still used today, the negative-positive system – an essentially reproductive process. It is not only books, prints and posters that use this process; the printed circuit boards of modern computer boards are miniaturised by photo-polymerisation. The idea of photography came to Talbot when he was on holiday at Lake Como; he was using a camera lucida as an aid to drawing the scenery, and the thought came to him '…how charming it would be if it were possible to cause these natural images to imprint themselves durably and remain fixed upon the paper'. The result of his researches was the earliest known photographic negative on paper, taken in 1835 and showing one of the latticed oriel windows on the south front of Lacock Abbey. Talbot called his photographic process the Calotype, from the Greek 'kalos' meaning beautiful. There is now a museum at Lacock dedicated to 'the Father of Modern Photography'.

WILLIAM HENRY FOX TALBOT (1800-1877) L1015

CORSHAM, BOX TUNNEL 1904 51492

One of the engineering marvels of Wiltshire is the Box Tunnel through Box Hill west of Corsham, on the railway line between Chippenham and Bath. The tunnel is 1.83 miles (2,950 metres) in length, and descends a 1 in 100 gradient from the east. It was built by Isambard Kingdom Brunel between 1838 and 1841 and was a highly dangerous engineering project due to its length and the difficult underlying strata – around 100 workers died during its construction. The work had to be divided into six isolated sections, but when the tunnel was finished and the two ends were joined, there was less than 2 inches (50 mm) error in their alignment. Brunel designed the tunnel's western portal, near Box, in a grand, classical style; this view shows the more modest eastern portal at the Corsham end.

In St Bartholomew's churchyard in Corsham is the gravestone of Sarah Jarvis. The inscription on her gravestone records her being in the 107th year of her age when she died in 1753, and that 'some time before her death she had fresh teeth'.

An architectural treasure of Corsham is the complex of Lady Margaret Hungerford Almshouses and Schoolroom at Pound Pill. The widow of Sir Edward Hungerford of Corsham Court who commanded the Parliamentarian forces in Wiltshire during the Civil War, Lady Margaret founded and endowed the almshouses in 1668 to shelter six poor people (later increased to eight) whilst the school provided free education for ten needy children. The almshouse complex is open to the public as an example of social provision in the past, including the old schoolroom, complete with its original 17th-century furnishings; as well as box pews and benches for the pupils, these include the imposing pulpit desk where the master sat at a vantage point high above his pupils, with an unusual assistant master's seat built into its front.

CORSHAM, THE ALMSHOUSES 1906 54353

Did You Know?
WILTSHIRE
A MISCELLANY

CASTLE COMBE, THE VILLAGE 1904 51508

North-west of Chippenham is Castle Combe which in medieval times was a weaving centre famous for the manufacture of a red and white cloth called 'Castlecombe'. Nowadays this picturesque village is often used as a film location. The musical film 'Dr Dolittle' starring Rex Harrison was filmed there in 1966, when the set decorators transformed it into the fishing village of Puddle-by-the-Marsh, with the By Brook widened to resemble a harbour. In more recent years Castle Combe was used as a location in the feature films 'Stardust', 'The Wolfman' and 'War Horse'. St Andrew's Church in the village is the home of the Castle Combe Clock, one of the very few English medieval clocks that are still in use. It also has an unusual medieval font, which was made with a stone book-rest on the side of the bowl so the priest could put down his service book during baptisms, allowing him to have both hands free to deal with the baby. This is a rare example of such a feature in an English church.

Did You Know?
WILTSHIRE
A MISCELLANY

Looming impressively above Malmesbury's medieval market cross in this view is Malmesbury Abbey, where the historian William of Malmesbury was a monk in the 12th century. In his work 'De Gesta Regum Anglorum' ('The Deeds of the Kings of England'), he tells the tale of Eilmer, the flying monk of Malmesbury, who can be claimed as the country's first aviator! Eilmer was a young monk at the abbey in the early 11th century who was interested in mathematics, astrology and the mechanics of flight. He made some wings and jumped from a tower, and apparently achieved a gliding flight of some reasonable distance, but he broke both his legs when he crashed to the ground. However he survived his injuries, although he was lame for the rest of his life. Eilmer is also known as Oliver, due to a scribe's miscopying of his name in the past, and the place in the town where he is supposed to have landed is known as Oliver's Lane after him. He is also commemorated with a modern stained glass window in the abbey.

MALMESBURY, THE MARKET CROSS 1924 76146

Did You Know?
WILTSHIRE
A MISCELLANY

Cricklade is Wiltshire's most northerly town, and the only town in the county that is sited beside the River Thames. Its name means 'the crossing place by the hill', from 'cruc' (hill) and 'gelad' (crossing), referring to its location where the Roman road called Ermin Street crossed the Thames on its route between Gloucester and Silchester. Cricklade is famous for the large nature reserve of North Meadow situated between the Rivers Thames and Churn. Winter flooding of the land has created a unique habitat for the Snake's Head Fritillary (Fritillaria meleagris), a species of flowering plant in the family Liliaceae that was once abundant in the UK, but is now rare in its wild state; North Meadow is one of the most notable sites in the country where it is found.

The highest town in Wiltshire is the aptly named Highworth, located on a hill at 436ft (133m) above sea level, north-east of Swindon. Highworth was once of much greater significance than Swindon, which is now Wiltshire's biggest conurbation – in fact, Swindon's first postal address was 'Swindon, near Highworth'!

HIGHWORTH, HIGH STREET
1911 H157301

SWINDON, MEN LEAVING THE GREAT WESTERN RAILWAY WORKS 1913 S254607

Swindon was just a quiet market town until the 1830s. Then Isambard Kingdom Brunel and Daniel Gooch established the Great Western Railway locomotion workshops to the north of the old town, along with housing for the workers, making Swindon a centre for heavy industry and engineering. At its height the GWR Works employed over 14,000 people, but this important part of the town's history came to an end in the 1980s when they closed. Most of the old Works buildings have now been converted into a Designer Outlet shopping village, but one on Kemble Drive houses the STEAM museum of the Great Western Railway that celebrates the story of locomotive manufacture at the GWR Works and the men and women who worked there. In pride of place is the 'Caerphilly Castle', a magnificent example of the locomotives that were built at Swindon, displayed in pristine glory in 'ex-works' condition, with gleaming brass and paintwork. An intriguing exhibit in the museum is Isambard Kingdom Brunel's walking stick, which unfolded to make a measuring stick 7ft ¼ inch long (2.14m) that he could use to check that the pioneering broad gauge of that size used by the GWR track had been laid correctly.

SWINDON, REGENT STREET 1967 S254065

In the background of this photograph of Regent Street is Swindon's old Town Hall, which is now used as a dance studio. In front of it stands the Cenotaph, seen behind the white shop awning in this view, which was unveiled in 1920 to commemorate the fallen of the First World War. Shortly before it was built, in 1919, this part of the town was the scene of Swindon's 'flagpole riot', when the town councillors decided to pay £200 to erect a tall flagpole with a gilded top-piece outside the Town Hall as part of the peace celebrations at the end of the war. The townspeople felt that the money could be better spent providing help for ex-servicemen, and the flagpole was burnt down by protestors.

Fleming Way in Swindon is named after Harold Fleming, the footballer who played for Swindon Town from 1907 to 1924, and who was capped for England eleven times.

Queen's Park was laid out in the centre of Swindon, close to Regent Circus and the Town Hall, in two phases between 1949 and 1964 and was officially opened in 1953, the year of the coronation of Queen Elizabeth II. The man credited with creating the park from a former claypit and area of derelict land is Maurice Williams, who was Swindon's General Superintendent of Parks from 1949 to 1975 and is commemorated with a plaque on the wall at the entrance to the Garden of Remembrance off Groundwell Road. The plaque's wording reads 'If you would see his monument, look around', echoing the inscription in London's St Paul's Cathedral over the tomb of its architect, Sir Christopher Wren – who was himself a Wiltshire man, born in 1632 at East Knoyle in the extreme south of Wiltshire, where his father was the rector.

A landmark of Swindon's skyline is the tower and broached spire of Christ Church in Cricklade Street, the parish church of the Old Town, which was designed by the famous church architect Sir George Gilbert Scott and built 1850-51. It is affectionately known locally as 'The Old Lady on the Hill'. The poet John Betjeman wrote a poem celebrating the famous peal of bells from this well-loved building, 'On Hearing the Full Peal of Ten Bells from Christ Church, Swindon, Wilts'.

The best-selling novel 'The Curious Incident of the Dog in the Night-time' by Mark Haddon, which won the 2003 Whitbread Book of the Year award, is set in Swindon.

The Richard Jefferies Museum and House at Marlborough Road in Coate, south-east of Swindon, commemorates the life and work of the respected writer and naturalist Richard Jefferies, who was born in the museum building, then a farmhouse, in 1848. He recorded his childhood memories of life in the countryside around mid 19th-century Swindon in a series of novels, most notably 'Bevis – The Story of a Boy'.

Did You Know? WILTSHIRE A MISCELLANY

WOOTTON BASSETT, THE MARKET, HIGH STREET 1919 W171507

Wootton Bassett is now known as 'Royal Wootton Bassett', after being granted royal patronage by Queen Elizabeth II in 2011. This was in recognition of the role it played in the military funeral repatriations of men and women of the British Armed Forces who died on active service in Iraq and Afghanistan that passed through the town between 2007 and 2011 from nearby RAF Lyneham, when local people lined the streets in huge numbers to show their respects. In the background of this busy view of its High Street in 1919 is the old Town Hall, erected around 1690, whose half-timbered upper storey is supported on fifteen columns. This quaint building now houses a local history museum.

Did You Know?
WILTSHIRE
A MISCELLANY

North-west of Swindon is Purton, where the Church of St Mary is unusual in having a central tower with a spire and a second tower at the western end. It is one of only three parish churches in England to have both a spire and a tower, the other two being at Wanborough, also in Wiltshire and near Swindon, and Ormskirk in Lancashire.

Just off the A4361 between Wroughton and Avebury is Broad Hinton. In the village church of St Peter ad Vincula is the impressive but curious monument to Sir Thomas Wroughton (d 1597) and his wife Lady Anne Wroughton, showing them kneeling in prayer with their children represented on the frieze below. The curious thing is that all the figures on the monument are handless, except Lady Anne's. The explanation is that Sir Thomas returned home one day to find his wife reading the Bible instead of preparing his meal, which angered him so much that he snatched the book from her and flung it into the fire. His wife managed to retrieve it but she burnt her hands badly in the process, whereupon Sir Thomas's hands and those of his children promptly withered away as a punishment for his blasphemy. The monument shows Lady Anne clutching her Bible, which has a corner missing to show where it was burnt.

Another unusual feature is found in St Mary's Church at Bishops Cannings, near Devizes, in the form of a meditation or confessional pew, similar to a single box pew with a small door and a desk opposite the seat. The back panel is decorated with a large painted 'Hand of Meditation', thought to be 15th-century, divided up with Latin inscriptions in the form of moral proverbs and admonitory phrases, such as 'Thou shalt quickly be forgotten by thy friends', 'He to whom thou leavest thy goods will seldom do anything for thee', and 'Thy end is miserable'.

Did You Know?
WILTSHIRE
A MISCELLANY

DEVIZES, THE BEAR HOTEL AND THE MARKET CROSS 1898 42301

The pretty town of Devizes is very near the centre of the county. It did not come into being until after the Norman Conquest when a castle was built there, located on the boundaries of the Bishop of Salisbury's manors of Rowde, Cannings and Potterne, which gave the settlement its name – from 'ad divisas', meaning 'at the boundaries'. The town had become known as just 'Divisas' by the 14th century. Devizes Castle was originally a Norman motte and bailey fortification, but was rebuilt in the early 12th century. It later fell into ruin, and the Devizes Castle that stands in the town today is a 19th-century romantic reconstruction. Devizes is noted for its Georgian architecture and spacious market place, which is the largest in the west of England. It was once one of the premier corn markets in the kingdom, a fact reflected by the statue of Ceres, the Roman goddess of agriculture, grain and harvests, that stands atop the handsome Corn Exchange in the market place (seen in the centre of this view), where local farmers came to sell their grain to the corn merchants.

Another feature of the market place in Devizes is the Market Cross, built in 1814. A lengthy inscription on a panel of the Cross tells the cautionary tale of Ruth Pierce of Potterne, just south of Devizes, who was struck down dead in the market place for dishonesty. The tale goes that in 1753 Ruth and two other women agreed to divide the cost of a sack of wheat between them. Their payment was found to be three pence short of the price asked, but all three protested that they had paid their correct share. Ruth then went one better and declared that she wished to drop down dead if she was lying. She did just that, and the missing money was found clutched in her hand.

Potterne has some wonderful ancient buildings, including the 15th-century timber-framed Porch House on the left of this view. Potterne people are known as 'Lambs', an ironic nickname given to them because of their reputation for boisterous and unruly behaviour in the 19th century, when the men of the village were notorious for hooliganism.

POTTERNE, OLD HOUSES AND THE CHURCH 1898 42321

Did You Know?
WILTSHIRE
A MISCELLANY

DEVIZES, THE CAEN HILL FLIGHT 1898 42320

The Kennet and Avon Canal runs across Wiltshire as part of its 87-mile route linking the Thames to the Bristol Channel. The 57-mile section connecting the Kennet and Avon Navigations was completed in 1810 and included the construction of 29 locks within just 2 miles which brought the canal to Devizes, perched on a hill above the Avon valley. Part of the Devizes 29 is this impressive set of 16 locks at Caen Hill, considered by many to be the finest series of locks in Britain. On the eastern side of the county is the Crofton Pumping Station near Great Bedwyn where water is pumped up to the summit pound (the highest point) of the canal where it runs through Savernake Forest. The pumping station now uses electric pumps, but the steam-driven beam engines that powered the pumping equipment when it was first built have been preserved, and are operated at special 'steaming weekends' in the summer. The Number 1 engine, built by Boulton & Watt and installed in 1812, is the oldest operational steam-driven beam engine in the world still in its original engine house and doing the job for which it was originally installed.

Savernake Forest is owned by the Earl of Cardigan, and as such is Britain's only privately-owned forest, although the Forestry Commission manages it under a long-term lease. The forest is crossed by great avenues of stately beech trees that were laid out by Lancelot 'Capability' Brown for the then owner in the 1790s. The most notable of these is the Grand Avenue that runs through the heart of the forest – it is just over 4 miles long and is listed in the Guinness Book of Records as the longest tree-lined avenue in Britain. Savernake contains a remarkable number of exceptionally large and ancient trees, some of which have attained a great girth, because of the way the forest woodland has been managed over many centuries. This view shows one of the most famous, the 'Big Belly Oak' that stands beside the A346 road, which was included in the list of Fifty Great British Trees compiled in 2012. It is over 1,000 years old, and has a girth of over 36ft (11m). Since this photograph was taken in the 1950s, the Big Belly Oak has been fitted with a metal corset to prevent it splitting in half.

SAVERNAKE FOREST, THE BIG BELLY OAK c1955 S66082

Did You Know?
WILTSHIRE
A MISCELLANY

MARLBOROUGH, HIGH STREET 1907 57846

Marlborough boasts one of the widest high streets in the country, eminently suited to busy market days in the past. This 1907 view is looking east towards the recently built Town Hall. The odd little building on the right hand side of the street was the old town lock-up, which was demolished in the 1920s as a traffic hazard. St Mary's Church is in the distance, where the north wall of the tower bears the marks of shot from Royalist guns, battle scars from a Civil War action in 1642 after King Charles I sent Lord Digby to take the Parliamentarian town. The people of Marlborough refused to surrender without a fight, but despite their defiance the Royalists successfully captured and looted the town. At the other end of the High Street is the Church of St Peter and St Paul; King Henry VIII's great statesman Thomas Wolsey (1473-1530) was ordained as a priest there in 1498, later to become a cardinal and the king's Lord Chancellor. The church became redundant in 1974, and has now been converted into an Arts Centre.

Some sources claim that Marlborough is named after 'Maerl's Barrow', the prehistoric tumulus that stands in the grounds of Marlborough College. There is an old legend that it is the burial mound of Merlin, the magician of the King Arthur tales, as recalled in the motto on Marlborough Town Council's coat of arms, 'Ubi nunc sapientis ossa Merlini' – 'Where now are the bones of wise Merlin'. However, Marlborough's name probably comes from 'marle burg', meaning 'the town on chalk'.

North-east of Marlborough is Aldbourne, where a strange bird was seen on the village pond many years ago. No one knew what it was, so the oldest inhabitant of the village was summoned to identify it. He pronounced it to be a Dabchick, the common name for the Little Grebe – and Aldbourne people have been known as 'Dabchicks' ever since! By contrast, people from nearby Ramsbury are known as 'Bulldogs'. This view of Ramsbury shows the ancient Wych Elm tree that was a landmark of the village for centuries. It died and was felled in the 1980s, and was replaced with an oak tree.

RAMSBURY, THE ELM TREE IN THE HIGH STREET 1906 57195x

Did You Know?
WILTSHIRE
A MISCELLANY

WARMINSTER, MARKET PLACE c1965 W261057

In the west of the county is Warminster, probably named after the River Were that runs through the town. William Cobbett was very complimentary about the place in his 'Rural Rides' in 1826, writing that it is 'a very nice town: everything belonging to it is solid and good'. One of Warminster's historic industries is glovemaking, and fine leather gloves are still handcrafted in the town by the Dents company at its modern factory in Furnax Lane, where there is a factory shop and also a fascinating Glove Museum. Dents made the gloves for Queen Elizabeth II to wear at her coronation in 1953, and one of those is now on display in the museum – as well one of the gloves worn by Queen Elizabeth I at her coronation in 1559! The Dents Glove Museum includes examples of gloves from the 16th, 17th, 18th and 19th centuries, many of which were owned by famous people including King Charles I, Queen Victoria, and Admiral Lord Nelson – the latter complete with a blood stain. The museum also holds the world's smallest hand-knitted gloves – each glove is no bigger than a thumbnail.

Visits to the Glove Museum can only be made by prior appointment – telephone 01985 212291 for information and to book a visit.

Did You Know?
WILTSHIRE
A MISCELLANY

Another item of clothing worn by King Charles I can be seen at Longleat House, west of Warminster, where the pale blue silk sleeved waistcoat the king wore to his execution in 1649 is on display in the Great Hall. The ancestral home of the Marquesses of Bath, Longleat was built by Sir John Thynne between 1568 and 1580 and was one of the great 'prodigy houses' of the Elizabethan age, sometimes described as the first true Renaissance house in England. It was the first stately home to be opened to the public on a commercial basis, in 1949, and when the famous safari park opened in its grounds in 1966 it was the first drive-though safari park outside Africa. The visitor attractions in the grounds of Longleat House include the world's longest hedge maze, which extends over 1½ acres with 1.69 miles of pathway. Over 16,000 yew trees make up the five miles of hedging of this monster and very complex maze. The hedges have two main trims twice a year – a job that takes the team of gardeners over a month each time!

LONGLEAT HOUSE c1960 L190002

Did You Know?
WILTSHIRE
A MISCELLANY

In the extreme south-western corner of Wiltshire at Stourton are the famous **Stourhead Gardens** that were laid out around Stourhead House in the 18th century and are now in the care of the National Trust. Henry Hoare had **Stourhead** House built in Palladian style between 1718 and 1724. In 1741 Henry Hoare the younger returned from the Grand Tour particularly impressed by what he had seen in Italy. He had become converted to the idea of 'educating' nature, using and modifying the natural contours to produce pleasing compositions. This inspired him to create one of England's great gardens.

Influenced by artists such as Claude and Poussin, Henry Hoare set about creating their vision of an 'Arcadian' landscape. The lake was created in 1744 with the intention that a walk round its shores would be an allegory of Aeneas's journey after he fled from the fall of Troy in Greek mythology. To make his vision a reality, Hoare had a series of classical-style buildings constructed around the lake, including the Pantheon, the Temple of Flora and the Temple of Apollo, inspired by the original at Baalbek in the Lebanon.

However, the building that stands at the entrance to the gardens, seen in the foreground of this view (opposite), with the Pantheon in the background, is firmly English in both design and history – it is the medieval High Cross that was erected in Bristol in 1373 to mark the granting of a charter to the city by King Edward III. It stood in centre of Bristol, at the junction of High Street, Broad Street, Wine Street and Corn Street, until the 18th century when it was considered a traffic hazard, and was re-erected elsewhere in the city. In 1762 it was dismantled again and left in pieces for some time before being offered to Henry Hoare for his gardens at Stourhead, where it was re-erected in 1765.

**STOURHEAD, THE PLEASURE GARDENS AND THE BRISTOL CROSS
c1965** S741093

A short distance north up the B3092 from Stourhead is Maiden Bradley, close to the border with Somerset. The village has a pretty name with a not-so-pretty derivation. The 'Bradley' part of its name comes from Old English words meaning 'a clearing in a wood', whilst the 'Maiden' part derives from the hospital that was founded near the village in the 12th century for young women suffering from leprosy on the site that later became an Augustinian priory.

WILTON HOUSE, THE DOUBLE CUBE ROOM 1919 68932

West of Salisbury is Wilton House, a magnificent Palladian mansion that is one of England's great houses. It stands on the site of the old Wilton Abbey whose estate was granted to the 1st Earl of Pembroke in 1544 after its dissolution, and his descendants have lived there ever since. Much of the earlier house was destroyed by a fire in 1647, and it was rebuilt for the 4th Earl of Pembroke to the designs of the great architect Inigo Jones. A famous feature of Wilton House is the spectacular 'Double Cube Room', 60ft (18m) long, 30ft (9m) wide and 30ft (9m) high, one of the most lavishly decorated rooms in the history of interior design, which was specially designed by Inigo Jones to house Sir Anthony van Dyck's portraits of the Herbert family. Wilton House is set in 21 acres of landscaped parkland and gardens. These include the Italian Garden, where the closing credit sequences for each episode of the 'Blackadder II' television series were filmed (the Elizabethan series), where Edmund Blackadder strolls through the formal gardens whilst being pursued by an annoying lute-playing minstrel.

Did You Know?
WILTSHIRE
A MISCELLANY

Salisbury is Wiltshire's only city, centred around its glorious medieval cathedral. The main body of the cathedral was completed between 1220 and 1260, in one Gothic style, Early English, which gives it a unique symmetry and unity of architectural design. It was the vision of Bishop Richard Poore, who is represented by one of the 69 statues on the west front, the second from the left in the bottom row. He is shown holding a model of the cathedral, but without the soaring spire that now adorns it – that was not part of the original design and was added later, completed by 1334; at 404ft (123m) high it is the tallest spire in England. There is a tradition that the cathedral has 365 windows to match the number of days and 8,760 pillars to match the number of hours in a year. In the north nave aisle in the cathedral is the oldest working mechanical clock in Europe, which dates from 1386, although it is quite primitive – it has no face, and only strikes the hours. Another treasure of the cathedral is one of the four original copies of the Magna Carta, which is displayed in the Chapter House.

SALISBURY, THE CATHEDRAL NORTH WEST 1887 19743

SALISBURY, POULTRY CROSS AND SILVER STREET 1906 56359

Reminders of the produce sold in various parts of the city in medieval times are found in a number of Salisbury's old street names as such as Fish Row, Ox Row, Salt Lane and Oatmeal Row, as well as the beautiful hexagonal Poultry Cross that stands in the city centre at the junction of Butcher Row and Minster Street. This famous landmark dates from the 15th century and is the only survivor of Salisbury's four medieval market crosses. It marked the area that was reserved for the selling of poultry and vegetables.

Peeping over the rooftops in the background of this view is the tower of the church of St Thomas of Canterbury. Inside the church is a remarkable and complete medieval Doom painting, dating from the 1470s. This amazing painting was whitewashed over in the 1590s and not discovered until 1881, when it was restored. Christ sits in judgement at the centre, with the blessed on His right hand and the damned to His left; the Devil waits below – and bishops are among those entering the mouth of hell!

Did You Know?
WILTSHIRE
A MISCELLANY

The atmospheric Haunch of Venison pub in Minster Street is probably the oldest and smallest pub in Salisbury. In 1911 a severed, mummified human hand was discovered in a wall of the building during renovation work. It was clutching some old playing cards and was reputed to be the hand of a man in the 18th century who was caught cheating whilst playing cards with a butcher from nearby Butcher Row, whereupon the angry butcher chopped off his hand with his knife. The grisly relic was displayed in a glass case in the pub until 2010, when it was stolen. However, a replica of the hand can still be seen there – and the handless card player's ghost is said to haunt the building!

The King's House in Salisbury Cathedral Close now houses the Salisbury and South Wiltshire Museum, but on 2nd November 1483 it was where King Richard III was lodging when he had Henry Stafford, 2nd Duke of Buckingham beheaded in Salisbury's Market Square for treason – afterwards, Buckingham's head was brought there for King Richard to see. Before his execution the Duke was imprisoned in the Blue Boar Inn, which stood on the site now occupied by the Debenhams department store in Blue Boar Row – and his ghost is said to haunt the store to this day. One of the treasures of the Salisbury and South Wiltshire Museum is the Salisbury Giant. He stands over 12ft (3.66m) tall and is a unique survival of life in the medieval city, when he was paraded in the streets by the Salisbury Guild of Tailors as a pageant figure during their annual celebration on the eve of the feast of St John (Midsummer's Day). In later times the Giant was also paraded through the city on occasions of public celebration, such as coronations or jubilees. He passed to the Museum in 1873 and was still taken out for public celebrations until 1979 when he was 'retired'. He now forms the centrepiece of the Salisbury gallery of the museum, accompanied by his companion, the Hob-Nob, a mischievous hobby-horse character who cavorted in front in the procession clearing the way for the Giant.

SPORTING WILTSHIRE

Wiltshire County Cricket Club was founded in 1893. Although the club plays its matches around the county, its main home is the County Ground at Trowbridge, which is also the home of Trowbridge Cricket Club. Club cricket has been played in Trowbridge since about 1840, and from 1850 onwards was played on a ground in Hilperton Road, where in 1856 Trowbridge CC took on the All England XI. Trowbridge CC moved to its present ground in Timbrell Street in the late 19th century, and the formal opening of the ground took place on 2nd May 1896, when a match was played between an XI captained by Dr W G Grace and a Trowbridge XI led by local MP Walter Long. A famous name in Wiltshire's cricket story is Trowbridge man Frederick William Stancomb (1861-1936), who became captain of Trowbridge CC when he was 19 and continued to captain the side for 50 years, the longest anyone has served as skipper of a cricket team. He first played cricket for the county team in 1904. Between 1880 and 1930 he took part in 1,510 innings and was declared not out 264 times; his highest score was 178. In 2001 F W Stancomb's daughter gave a substantial donation towards the cost of restoring the magnificent pavilion at Trowbridge Cricket Ground, seen here at it looked in 1907.

TROWBRIDGE, THE COUNTY CRICKET GROUND PAVILION 1907 57705

A famous name in sporting history is that of the Wiltshire athlete Walter Goodall George (1848-1943) of Calne, who held the world record for running the mile for nearly 30 years, from 1886 to 1915, with his time of 4:12¾ minutes – and he still holds a world record simply for holding the mile record longer than anyone else!

Swindon Town Football Club is the only Football League club in Wiltshire, known as The Robins, The Reds and The Town. Swindon Town FC had an extraordinary start in the Football League. After joining Division Three South as one of the founder members in 1920 the club won its first match, against Luton Town, by 9-1. This remains the club's highest ever win in the League. The most famous match in Swindon Town's history is probably the 1969 League Cup 3-1 victory over Arsenal at Wembley. Under player-manager Glen Hoddle Swindon Town achieved promotion to the Premier League for the 1993-94 season. Although the club were relegated at the end of the season, a notable achievement of their time in the top flight was holding Manchester United to a 2-2 draw. Swindon Town player John Trollope still holds the record for the most Swindon Town appearances, having played 889 first-team matches for the club between 1960 and 1980, and he also holds the record for the most English Football League appearances for one club, having played in 770 League games.

Salisbury Racecourse is a flat racing course to the south-west of the city, where fifteen race meetings a year are held between early May and mid-October. There has been racing at the course since the mid-16th century, and one of the most important fixtures of its early years was the King's Plate for 6-year-olds, which was awarded by King George I in 1723. The highest class race of Salisbury's season nowadays is the Sovereign Stakes in August, which is open to thoroughbred colts and geldings aged three years or older and run over a distance of 1 mile. The legendary jockey Lester Piggott rode in public for the first time at Salisbury Racecourse, in 1948.

QUIZ QUESTIONS

Answers on page 52.

1. This shows the County Flag of Wiltshire that was formally approved by Wiltshire Council on December 1st 2009. The green and white lines on the flag represent the grassy downs of Wiltshire and their underlying chalk, and the green and white circle around the bird represents the prehistoric stone circles of Stonehenge and Avebury – but what type of bird is it?

2. What is the highest point in Wiltshire?

3. In Wiltshire dialect, what is a 'gally-bagger', or 'gally-crow'?

4. What is the Marlborough Bucket and where can you see it?

5. According to the inscription on her gravestone in the grounds of Malmesbury Abbey, what dreadful fate befell Hannah Twynnoy, who died October 23rd 1703, aged 33?

6. The Great Western Railway was of great importance to Swindon's history. By what affectionate nickname was the GWR known?

Did You Know?
WILTSHIRE
A MISCELLANY

7. Which of King Henry VIII's six wives was a Wiltshire girl?

8. The streets of Chippenham fill with music and colour at the Spring Bank Holiday weekend during the annual Chippenham Folk Festival – but the town also hosts an annual rock and roll music festival too. What is it called, and why is it held at Chippenham?

9. Great Wishford is a village in the Wylye Valley, about 5 miles north-west of Salisbury. What do the people of Great Wishford do on 29th May each year, and why?

10. Why will you not find anyone at home if you knock on the door of this house in Trowbridge?

TROWBRIDGE, 4A ROUNDSTONE STREET 2004 T84723

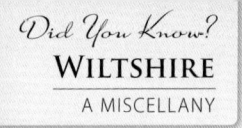

RECIPES

Wiltshire Plait

This is rather like a giant sausage roll and is good eaten either hot or cold. Use belly pork which has an equal amount of lean meat and fat, and a mature, well-flavoured Cheddar cheese. Serves 4.

275g/10oz belly pork, minced, or chopped into very small pieces
50g/2oz cooking apple, peeled, cored and chopped into small pieces
50g/2oz mature cheddar cheese, grated
50g/2oz onion, peeled and finely chopped
1 garlic clove, peeled and crushed or very finely chopped
5 tablespoonfuls finely chopped fresh broadleaf parsley
Salt and freshly ground black pepper
1 egg, beaten
350g/12oz prepared puff pastry

Pre-heat the oven to 220°C/425°F/Gas Mark 7 and grease a baking sheet.

Mix together the pork, apple, cheese, onion, garlic, parsley and half the beaten egg, and season well with salt and freshly ground black pepper.

Roll out the pastry to about 23-26cms (9-10 ins) square. Flour your hands and form the meat mixture into a loaf shape about 8 x 20cms (3 x 8ins) and lay it in the centre of the pastry square. Cut the pastry on either side of it into diagonal strips 1cm (½ inch) wide. Dampen the end of each strip, then fold the strips alternately over the meat loaf from side to side to create a plaited, lattice effect in a criss-cross pattern over the filling, sealing the ends down firmly to the pastry on the other side. Brush all over the pastry with the remaining beaten egg. Carefully slide the Plait onto a dampened baking sheet (this helps the pastry to puff) and bake in the pre-heated oven for 20 minutes, then reduce the oven temperature to 180°C/350°F/Gas Mark 4 and bake for a further 20-25 minutes.

Watercress Soup

Traditionally-grown watercress is cultivated in flowing watercourses of mineral-rich water of the highest purity, and the clear chalk streams of Wiltshire are ideal for growing it. Watercress beds were once prolific in Wiltshire and watercress is still produced by a few commercial growers in the county, such as John Hurd's Organic Watercress at Hill Deverill, south of Warminster, which supplies Waitrose stores, and Chalke Valley Watercress at Broadchalke, west of Salisbury. Watercress is a super-food packed with nutrients, with a distinctive peppery, slightly bitter, flavour. It can be eaten raw as a salad or in sandwiches or used to make a sauce to accompany freshwater fish, but is best known for making a delicious soup.

> 2-3 bunches or bags of watercress (approximately 200g/7oz total weight)
> 25g/1oz butter
> 1 medium sized onion, peeled and chopped
> 225g/8oz potatoes, peeled and chopped
> 1.2 litres/2 pints chicken or vegetable stock
> Salt and freshly ground black pepper
> Freshly grated nutmeg, to serve (optional)
> 125ml/4 fl oz single cream, crème fraîche or natural yogurt, to serve (optional)

Melt the butter in a large saucepan. Add the chopped onion and cook over a medium heat for 4-5 minutes, until soft and transparent but not browned. Add the chopped potatoes and cook for a further 4-5 minutes, stirring occasionally to prevent sticking, then add the stock. Chop through the bunches of watercress about one third from the leafy ends, and retain the leafy section for later. Roughly chop the stalks and any remaining leaves on them, and add to the pan – the stalks help flavour the soup. Bring the soup to the boil, then reduce the heat, cover the pan and simmer gently for about 20 minutes, until the potato pieces are soft and tender. Stir in the reserved watercress and allow to heat through for about 3 minutes. Remove the pan from the heat and allow the soup to cool for a few minutes, then liquidise with a blender or food processor. Return the soup to the rinsed out pan, reheat and season to taste with salt and freshly ground black pepper, and a little freshly grated nutmeg, if using. Serve, adding a swirl of single cream, crème fraîche or natural yogurt to each helping if liked.

QUIZ ANSWERS

1. A Great Bustard (Otis tarda) stands at the centre of the County Flag of Wiltshire. The Great Bustard was once common on Salisbury Plain but was hunted out of existence and became extinct in England in the 1830s. It has now been successfully re-introduced on the Plain as part of an intense breeding programme.

2. The highest point in Wiltshire is Milk Hill on the chalk downs near Alton Priors on the western edge of the Vale of Pewsey. At its highest point it reaches 294.19m (965ft 2ins) above sea level, pipping the adjacent Tan Hill for the title by just 26cms (10.2 ins), which rises to 293.93m (964ft 4ins) The measurements to establish which summit was the highest point in the county were carried out in 2009 by a team from the BBC's 'Countryfile' television programme using satellite GPS technology, accompanied by Paul Denyer from Ordnance Survey, who verified the measurements using similar equipment.

3. A 'gally-bagger', or 'gally-crow', is a scarecrow.

4. The Marlborough Bucket is an Iron Age burial bucket for cremated human remains, with decorations of grotesque animal forms and human heads on sheet bronze, which was found on the outskirts of Marlborough in 1807. It is one of the greatest archaeological treasures found in Wiltshire, and one of the finest examples of Celtic art from the British Isles. It can be seen in the Wiltshire Heritage Museum in Devizes.

5. Hannah was a maidservant at the White Lion Inn in Gloucester Street in Malmesbury when a travelling menagerie visited the inn, and she was killed when its tiger escaped and attacked her.

6. God's Wonderful Railway.

7. Jane Seymour (c1508-1537), King Henry's third wife, who was the mother of his son, Edward, but died soon after his birth. She was born at the Seymour family home of Wolfhall Manor near Burbage, much of which was demolished in the 1660s. Her father Sir John Seymour (d1590) was the Warden of Savernake Forest, and his tomb is in St Mary's Church at Great Bedwyn, where his effigy shows him in full armour with his feet resting on a lion.

8. Chippenham holds an Eddie Cochran Festival every April in remembrance of the American rock and roll singer Eddie Cochran, who tragically died on 17th April 1960 following a car accident on Rowden Hill the previous night, whilst travelling through Chippenham on his way back to London after playing at Bristol. The festival attracts a host of top British rock and roll bands celebrating the life of this popular singer, famous for hits such as 'C'mon Everybody' and 'Summertime Blues'.

9. Great Wishford is one of the few places in England that still observes Oak Apple Day on 29th May, which used to be celebrated all over the country to commemorate the restoration of King Charles II to the throne in 1660 following the Civil War. On 29th May each year the villagers of Great Wishford wake early and go into the nearby woods to gather oak branches. They then travel into Salisbury and hold a service in the cathedral, which ends with them shouting 'Grovely, Grovely, Grovely and all Grovely!' and dancing on the Cathedral Green. Why? To assert their ancient rights to collect firewood from Grovely Forest above the village!

10. The photograph on page 49 shows the side elevation of Number 4 Roundstone Street in Trowbridge – which is actually a trompe l'oeil façade that was painted on the blank wall of the building by local artist Roger Smith, and unveiled in 2003 to celebrate the Silver Jubilee of Trowbridge Civic Society. It is believed to be the largest trompe l'oeil in the country.

FRANCIS FRITH

PIONEER VICTORIAN PHOTOGRAPHER

Francis Frith, founder of the world-famous photographic archive, was a complex and multi-talented man. A devout Quaker and a highly successful Victorian businessman, he was philosophical by nature and pioneering in outlook. By 1855 he had already established a wholesale grocery business in Liverpool, and sold it for the astonishing sum of £200,000, which is the equivalent today of over £15,000,000. Now in his thirties, and captivated by the new science of photography, Frith set out on a series of pioneering journeys up the Nile and to the Near East.

INTRIGUE AND EXPLORATION

He was the first photographer to venture beyond the sixth cataract of the Nile. Africa was still the mysterious 'Dark Continent', and Stanley and Livingstone's historic meeting was a decade into the future. The conditions for picture taking confound belief. He laboured for hours in his wicker dark-room in the sweltering heat of the desert, while the volatile chemicals fizzed dangerously in their trays. Back in London he exhibited his photographs and was 'rapturously cheered' by members of the Royal Society. His reputation as a photographer was made overnight.

VENTURE OF A LIFE-TIME

By the 1870s the railways had threaded their way across the country, and Bank Holidays and half-day Saturdays had been made obligatory by Act of Parliament. All of a sudden the working man and his family were able to enjoy days out, take holidays, and see a little more of the world.

With typical business acumen, Francis Frith foresaw that these new tourists would enjoy having souvenirs to commemorate their days out. For the next thirty years he travelled the country by train and by pony and trap, producing fine photographs of seaside resorts and beauty spots that were keenly bought by millions of Victorians. These prints were painstakingly pasted into family albums and pored over during the dark nights of winter, rekindling precious memories of summer excursions. Frith's studio was soon supplying retail shops all over the country, and by 1890 F Frith & Co had become the greatest specialist photographic publishing company in the world, with over 2,000 sales outlets, and pioneered the picture postcard.

FRANCIS FRITH'S LEGACY

Francis Frith had died in 1898 at his villa in Cannes, his great project still growing. By 1970 the archive he created contained over a third of a million pictures showing 7,000 British towns and villages.

Frith's legacy to us today is of immense significance and value, for the magnificent archive of evocative photographs he created provides a unique record of change in the cities, towns and villages throughout Britain over a century and more. Frith and his fellow studio photographers revisited locations many times down the years to update their views, compiling for us an enthralling and colourful pageant of British life and character.

We are fortunate that Frith was dedicated to recording the minutiae of everyday life. For it is this sheer wealth of visual data, the painstaking chronicle of changes in dress, transport, street layouts, buildings, housing and landscape that captivates us so much today, offering us a powerful link with the past and with the lives of our ancestors.

Computers have now made it possible for Frith's many thousands of images to be accessed almost instantly. The archive offers every one of us an opportunity to examine the places where we and our families have lived and worked down the years. Its images, depicting our shared past, are now bringing pleasure and enlightenment to millions around the world a century and more after his death.

For further information visit: www.francisfrith.com

INTERIOR DECORATION

Frith's photographs can be seen framed and as giant wall murals in thousands of pubs, restaurants, hotels, banks, retail stores and other public buildings throughout Britain. These provide interesting and attractive décor, generating strong local interest and acting as a powerful reminder of gentler days in our increasingly busy and frenetic world.

FRITH PRODUCTS

All Frith photographs are available as prints and posters in a variety of different sizes and styles. In the UK we also offer a range of other gift and stationery products illustrated with Frith photographs, although many of these are not available for delivery outside the UK – see our web site for more information on the products available for delivery in your country.

THE INTERNET

Over 100,000 photographs of Britain can be viewed and purchased on the Frith web site. The web site also includes memories and reminiscences contributed by our customers, who have personal knowledge of localities and of the people and properties depicted in Frith photographs. If you wish to learn more about a specific town or village you may find these reminiscences fascinating to browse. Why not add your own comments if you think they would be of interest to others? See **www.francisfrith.com**

PLEASE HELP US BRING FRITH'S PHOTOGRAPHS TO LIFE

Our authors do their best to recount the history of the places they write about. They give insights into how particular towns and villages developed, they describe the architecture of streets and buildings, and they discuss the lives of famous people who lived there. But however knowledgeable our authors are, the story they tell is necessarily incomplete.

Frith's photographs are so much more than plain historical documents. They are living proofs of the flow of human life down the generations. They show real people at real moments in history; and each of those people is the son or daughter of someone, the brother or sister, aunt or uncle, grandfather or grandmother of someone else. All of them lived, worked and played in the streets depicted in Frith's photographs.

We would be grateful if you would give us your insights into the places shown in our photographs: the streets and buildings, the shops, businesses and industries. Post your memories of life in those streets on the Frith website: what it was like growing up there, who ran the local shop and what shopping was like years ago; if your workplace is shown tell us about your working day and what the building is used for now. Read other visitors' memories and reconnect with your shared local history and heritage. With your help more and more Frith photographs can be brought to life, and vital memories preserved for posterity, and for the benefit of historians in the future.

Wherever possible, we will try to include some of your comments in future editions of our books. Moreover, if you spot errors in dates, titles or other facts, please let us know, because our archive records are not always completely accurate—they rely on 140 years of human endeavour and hand-compiled records. You can email us using the contact form on the website.

Thank you!

For further information, trade, or author enquiries
please contact us at the address below:

**The Francis Frith Collection, 6 Oakley Business Park,
Wylye Road, Dinton, Wiltshire SP3 5EU.**

Tel: +44 (0)1722 716 376 Fax: +44 (0)1722 716 881
e-mail: sales@francisfrith.co.uk **www.francisfrith.com**